Francis Frith's
East Grinstead

DAVID GOULD who is 56, has lived in East Grinstead since 1980, having moved there from a tiny country cottage, home since 1955, between Crowhurst and Blindley Heath in Surrey. He spent his early childhood in Cardiff, attending Allensbank School there. After moving to Surrey he spent five years at Tandridge Primary School, three at Lingfield Secondary and two at Carshalton College of Further Education. Since 1974 he has had several books published, mainly on the subject of railways in south-east England - his special interest - and three dealing with East Grinstead in old photographs. He enjoys cycling, and photography when he can find anything worth photographing!

Photographic Memories

Francis Frith's
East Grinstead

———————

David Gould

FRITH
BOOK Co

First published in the United Kingdom in 2002 by
Frith Book Company Ltd

Paperback Edition 2002
ISBN 1-85937-138-8

Hardback Edition 2002
ISBN 1-85937-349-6

British Library Cataloguing in Publication Data

Francis Frith's East Grinstead
David Gould

Frith Book Company Ltd
Frith's Barn, Teffont,
Salisbury, Wiltshire SP3 5QP
Tel: +44 (0) 1722 716 376
Email: info@francisfrith.co.uk
www.francisfrith.co.uk

Printed and bound in Great Britain

Front Cover: East Grinstead, High Street 1933 85523

Contents

Francis Frith: Victorian Pioneer   7

Frith's Archive - A Unique Legacy   10

East Grinstead - An Introduction   12

A Tour of the Town   16

Felbridge   78

Dunnings Mill and Saint Hill Green   80

Forest Row   82

Hartfield   86

Index   89

Free Mounted Print Voucher   93

Francis Frith: *Victorian Pioneer*

FRANCIS FRITH, Victorian founder of the world-famous photographic archive, was a complex and multi-talented man. A devout Quaker and a highly successful Victorian businessman, he was both philosophic by nature and pioneering in outlook.

By 1855 Francis Frith had already established a wholesale grocery business in Liverpool, and sold it for the astonishing sum of £200,000, which is the equivalent today of over £15,000,000. Now a multi-millionaire, he was able to indulge his passion for travel. As a child he had pored over travel books written by early explorers, and his fancy and imagination had been stirred by family holidays to the sublime mountain regions of Wales and Scotland. 'What a land of spirit-stirring and enriching scenes and places!' he had written. He was to return to these scenes of grandeur in later years to 'recapture the thousands of vivid and tender memories', but with a different purpose. Now in his thirties, and captivated by the new science of photography, Frith set out on a series of pioneering journeys to the Nile regions that occupied him from 1856 until 1860.

Intrigue and Adventure

He took with him on his travels a specially-designed wicker carriage that acted as both dark-room and sleeping chamber. These far-flung journeys were packed with intrigue and adventure. In his life story, written when he was sixty-three, Frith tells of being held captive by bandits, and of fighting 'an awful midnight battle to the very point of surrender with a deadly pack of hungry, wild dogs'. Sporting flowing Arab costume, Frith arrived at Akaba by camel seventy years before Lawrence, where he encountered 'desert princes and rival sheikhs, blazing with jewel-hilted swords'.

During these extraordinary adventures he was assiduously exploring the desert regions bordering the Nile and patiently recording the antiquities and peoples with his camera. He was the first photographer to venture beyond the sixth cataract. Africa was still the mysterious 'Dark Continent', and Stanley and Livingstone's historic meeting was a decade into the future. The conditions for picture taking confound belief. He laboured for hours in his wicker dark-room in the sweltering heat of the desert, while the volatile chemicals fizzed dangerously in their trays. Often he was forced to work in remote tombs and caves where conditions were cooler. Back in London he exhibited his photographs and was 'rapturously cheered' by members of the Royal Society. His reputation as a photographer was made overnight. An eminent modern historian has likened their impact on the population of the time to that on our own generation of the first photographs taken on the surface of the moon.

Venture of a Life-Time

Characteristically, Frith quickly spotted the opportunity to create a new business as a specialist publisher of photographs. He lived in an era of immense and sometimes violent change. For the poor in the early part of Victoria's reign work was a drudge and the hours long, and people had precious little free time to enjoy themselves. Most had no transport other than a cart or gig at their disposal, and had not travelled far beyond the boundaries of their own town or village. However,

by the 1870s, the railways had threaded their way across the country, and Bank Holidays and half-day Saturdays had been made obligatory by Act of Parliament. All of a sudden the ordinary working man and his family were able to enjoy days out and see a little more of the world.

With characteristic business acumen, Francis Frith foresaw that these new tourists would enjoy having souvenirs to commemorate their days out. In 1860 he married Mary Ann Rosling and set out with the intention of photographing every city, town and village in Britain. For the next thirty years he travelled the country by train and by pony and trap, producing fine photographs of seaside resorts and beauty spots that were keenly bought by millions of Victorians. These prints were painstakingly pasted into family albums and pored over during the dark nights of winter, rekindling precious memories of summer excursions.

The Rise of Frith & Co

Frith's studio was soon supplying retail shops all over the country. To meet the demand he gathered about him a small team of photographers, and published the work of independent artist-photographers of the calibre of Roger Fenton and Francis Bedford. In order to gain some understanding of the scale of Frith's business one only has to look at the catalogue issued by Frith & Co in 1886: it runs to some 670 pages, listing not only many thousands of views of the British Isles but also many photographs of most European countries, and China, Japan, the USA and Canada – note the sample page shown above from the hand-written *Frith & Co* ledgers detailing pictures taken. By 1890 Frith had created the greatest specialist photographic publishing company in the world,

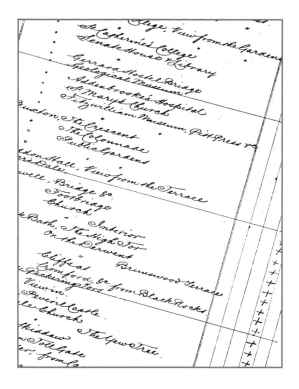

Frith's death, a new card measuring 5.5 x 3.5 inches became the standard format, but it was not until 1902 that the divided back came into being, with address and message on one face and a full-size illustration on the other. *Frith & Co* were in the vanguard of postcard development, and Frith's sons Eustace and Cyril continued their father's monumental task, expanding the number of views offered to the public and recording more and more places in Britain, as the coasts and countryside were opened up to mass travel.

Francis Frith died in 1898 at his villa in Cannes, his great project still growing. The archive he created continued in business for another seventy years. By 1970 it contained over a third of a million pictures of 7,000 cities, towns and villages. The massive photographic record Frith has left to us stands as a living monument to a special and very remarkable man.

with over 2,000 outlets – more than the combined number that Boots and WH Smith have today! The picture on the right shows the *Frith & Co* display board at Ingleton in the Yorkshire Dales. Beautifully constructed with mahogany frame and gilt inserts, it could display up to a dozen local scenes.

Postcard Bonanza

The ever-popular holiday postcard we know today took many years to develop. In 1870 the Post Office issued the first plain cards, with a pre-printed stamp on one face. In 1894 they allowed other publishers' cards to be sent through the mail with an attached adhesive halfpenny stamp. Demand grew rapidly, and in 1895 a new size of postcard was permitted called the court card, but there was little room for illustration. In 1899, a year after

Frith's Archive: *A Unique Legacy*

FRANCIS FRITH'S legacy to us today is of immense significance and value, for the magnificent archive of evocative photographs he created provides a unique record of change in 7,000 cities, towns and villages throughout Britain over a century and more. Frith and his fellow studio photographers revisited locations many times down the years to update their views, compiling for us an enthralling and colourful pageant of British life and character.

We tend to think of Frith's sepia views of Britain as nostalgic, for most of us use them to conjure up memories of places in our own lives with which we have family associations. It often makes us forget that to Francis Frith they were records of daily life as it was actually being lived in the cities, towns and villages of his day. The Victorian age was one of great and often bewildering change for ordinary people, and though the pictures evoke an impression of slower times, life was as busy and hectic as it is today.

We are fortunate that Frith was a photographer of the people, dedicated to recording the minutiae of everyday life. For it is this sheer wealth of visual data, the painstaking chronicle of changes in dress, transport, street layouts, buildings, housing, engineering and landscape that captivates us so much today. His remarkable images offer us a powerful link with the past and with the lives of our ancestors.

Today's Technology

Computers have now made it possible for Frith's many thousands of images to be accessed almost instantly. In the Frith archive today, each photograph is carefully 'digitised' then stored on a CD Rom. Frith archivists can locate a single photograph amongst thousands within seconds. Views can be catalogued and sorted under a variety of categories of place and content to the immediate benefit of researchers.

Inexpensive reference prints can be created for them at the touch of a mouse button, and a wide range of books and other printed materials assembled and published for a wider, more general readership - in the next twelve months over a hundred Frith local history titles will be published! The day-to-day workings of the archive are very different from how they were in Francis Frith's time: imagine the herculean task of sorting through eleven tons of glass negatives as Frith had to do to locate a particular sequence of pictures! Yet

THE FRANCIS FRITH COLLECTION
Photographic publishers since 1860

HOME | PHOTO SEARCH | BOOKS | PORTFOLIO | GALLERY   MY CART
Products | History | Other Collections | Contact us | Help?

your town,
your village

365,000 photographs of 7,000 towns and villages, taken between 1860 & 1970.

The Frith Archive
The Frith Archive is the remarkable legacy of its energetic and visionary founder. Today, the Frith archive is the only nationally important archive of its kind still in private ownership.

The Collection is world-renowned for the extraordinary quality of its images.

The Gallery
This month The Frith Gallery features images from "Frith's Egypt".

News...
Image update complete. An additional 5,000 images have been added and the quality of all images has now been improved.

Sample Chapters available. The first selection of sample chapters from the Frith Book Co.'s extensive range is now available. All are offered in Pdf format for easy downloading and viewing.

explore FRITH
Search thousands of photographs from one of the worlds' great archives.

Town search

County search
Select a county

the FRITHgallery

See Frith at www.francisfrith.co.uk

the archive still prides itself on maintaining the same high standards of excellence laid down by Francis Frith, including the painstaking cataloguing and indexing of every view.

It is curious to reflect on how the internet now allows researchers in America and elsewhere greater instant access to the archive than Frith himself ever enjoyed. Many thousands of individual views can be called up on screen within seconds on one of the Frith internet sites, enabling people living continents away to revisit the streets of their ancestral home town, or view places in Britain where they have enjoyed holidays. Many overseas researchers welcome the chance to view special theme selections, such as transport, sports, costume and ancient monuments.

We are certain that Francis Frith would have heartily approved of these modern developments in imaging techniques, for he himself was always working at the very limits of Victorian photographic technology.

The Value of the Archive Today

Because of the benefits brought by the computer, Frith's images are increasingly studied by social historians, by researchers into genealogy and ancestory, by architects, town planners, and by teachers and schoolchildren involved in local history projects.

In addition, the archive offers every one of us an opportunity to examine the places where we and our families have lived and worked down the years. Highly successful in Frith's own era, the archive is now, a century and more on, entering a new phase of popularity.

The Past in Tune with the Future

Historians consider the Francis Frith Collection to be of prime national importance. It is the only archive of its kind remaining in private ownership and has been valued at a million pounds. However, this figure is now rapidly increasing as digital technology enables more and more people around the world to enjoy its benefits.

Francis Frith's archive is now housed in an historic timber barn in the beautiful village of Teffont in Wiltshire. Its founder would not recognize the archive office as it is today. In place of the many thousands of dusty boxes containing glass plate negatives and an all-pervading odour of photographic chemicals, there are now ranks of computer screens. He would be amazed to watch his images travelling round the world at unimaginable speeds through network and internet lines.

The archive's future is both bright and exciting. Francis Frith, with his unshakeable belief in making photographs available to the greatest number of people, would undoubtedly approve of what is being done today with his lifetime's work. His photographs, depicting our shared past, are now bringing pleasure and enlightenment to millions around the world a century and more after his death.

East Grinstead - *An Introduction*

EAST GRINSTEAD is a North Sussex town that was founded in the 13th century. The name itself, which some outsiders find rather curious, is even older, referring to an area known as Grenestede, meaning 'a clearing in the forest' or 'green place'. In the 11th century it was called Grenestede, but by the 13th century it had become Estgrenested, to distinguish it from West Grinstead, a place south of Horsham.

The earliest part was the present High Street, made broad and expansive to allow plenty of space for markets and fairs. More building along London Road came in the 19th century, since when the town has greatly expanded in all directions, with new roads for residential development being added from the mid-19th century onwards.

It was in 1855 that the first photographs were taken in the town, these being by Joseph Cundall and Philip De La Motte, and by the 1860s one or two locally-based photographers had set up shop to produce portraits and street scenes. Francis Frith & Co seem to have been the first of the national

postcard-producing firms to photograph the town, this being in 1890 when the population of East Grinstead was about 5,500. Rival firms J Valentine and the Photochrom Co followed in their footsteps about ten years later, and after 1902, when view cards took off in popularity, the national firms vied with local publishers for sales. The town's local photographers tended to offer their customers cards incorporating real photographs, whereas the bigger studios tended to sell mass-produced printed cards.

In the years from 1902 to 1914 there was a picture postcard mania, and a wide range of subjects and themes were made into postcards. As it cost only one half penny to send cards, and as the postal service was so reliable, people used them to write brief messages making appointments for later the same day, or simply to say 'Just a few lines for now - will write at length later'. After the first World War, when the cost of postage went up to a penny, cards declined a little in popularity, but it did not stop the publication of new postcard views of East Grinstead. Frith photographers visited the town on eighteen separate occasions between 1890 and 1937, concentrating mainly on the High Street and London Road, which were the most picturesque parts of the town and those most likely to sell to the general public.

Only in 1907 and 1911 were other roads featured to any extent, and Blackwell Hollow, College Lane, Lewes Road, Moat Road, Ship Street, Station Road and St James's Road were all visited. For views of other roads such as Railway Approach, Queen's Road and Lingfield Road, one has to turn to local publishers such as William Page, who had his studio in Moat Road. One can imagine him glaring out of his window at the sight of the Frith photographer setting up his camera right outside Page's house one day in 1907. Page already faced enough competition from Arthur Harding, another local photographer who issued vast numbers of postcards.

After the second World War, the Frith company resumed its coverage of the town, Mr Trevor Sergeant making nine or ten visits between 1948 and 1967. During this period only the High Street and London Road were covered, with an occasional study of the Parish Church, the hospital and Sackville College, a Jacobean almshouse at the east end of the High Street. By 1965 the town was quite large, its population more than 16,000, and many buildings - some of poor quality but many that would have been worth keeping - had been demolished.

The earliest views of East Grinstead are the most interesting as records of vanished times, but they are not always thrilling pictorially. They tend to lack life and activity, with few people or vehicles to be seen. However, in defence of the Frith photographers, it must be said that there were far fewer people walking the streets of the town in 1890, and what few there were might not have registered on the emulsion if they moved too quickly across the line of sight - during this era photographic exposures were still long.

Of the pre-Great War batches the series taken in May 1914 are certainly the finest. The lighting is just right, with soft sunshine pervading every picture, and the composition - particularly that of photograph 66750 - is invariably superb; this particular view shows London Road with shops on one side, a tree overhanging the scene on the other, and is enlivened by the presence of several shoppers.

It was always helpful if the sun was shining, and the Frith photographers were usually lucky with the weather, though there were some years in which batches of photographs had to be taken without the benefit of sympathetic light. Such images can appear very dull, especially when reproduced as sepia half-tones. Originally, sepia was the most popular colour for postcards, but grew out-moded during the 1930s. F Frith & Co., however, seemed very committed to the sepia postcard, and went on producing them right up to the mid-1950s, after which (at last) real-photo cards started to appear. It was also Frith company practice to issue hand-tinted versions of some cards; these often looked very attractive but the colours were not always accurate.

Some local history photo books use postcards as source images for printing. Very often the results are fuzzy and devoid of detail. However, all the photographs in this book are reproduced not from Frith postcards but from the original archive photographic prints. As a result, the quality of reproduction and detail throughout is vastly superior. Perhaps the most exciting images are those from the 1960s, and in particular the batch taken in 1965 - few of these photographs seem ever

to have been issued as postcards and so are almost certainly being published here for the first time. The batch taken of the High Street and London Road on a late summer's day in September 1965 (E8101-18) is particularly good, showing crowds of shoppers and a variety of motor cars of the period.

According to the 1965 edition of 'East Grinstead - The Official Guide', the High Street has a distinct charm of its own, containing both Tudor and Jacobean buildings, the 'cathedral-like' Parish Church, and the 'peerless' Sackville College. The High Street is said to provide a shopping centre 'in which may be found the dignity of a past age'. In contrast, London Road has a 'glittering parade of modern shops' - an enthusiastic description that perhaps overstates the case a little. London Road nowadays has little or no charm, though it is certainly full of character, its haphazard frontages on the west side contrasting with the homogeneous line of shops on the east; even the late 19th-century buildings they replaced were not particularly handsome, though they did exude an air of prosperity and self-confidence.

When perusing scenes of the early 1900s there is always the great temptation to think, 'How peaceful

it all looks - what a beautiful town it was in those days when the streets weren't cluttered with traffic'. This, of course, is true up to a point, but would we really wish to have lived then? There was much poverty, tramps were prolific and the workhouse was never far away for many unfortunate people. Road surfaces were much rougher and muddier, and often covered with horse droppings, the smell of which was overpowering on hot days. Cars, too, were a hazard for pedestrians, sending up clouds of thick dust as they passed by. Traders were more versatile than now, providing multiple services from one shop. For example, they might offer tailoring and haircutting, or deal in bicycles, prams and gramophones. The lives of the upper classes were made more comfortable by servants, and even the lower middle-class townsman ususally employed at least one domestic servant. However, the Great War ensured that things would never be the same again for anyone.

Street furniture is always worth looking at in old photographs, being sparse and invariably tastefully designed. Gas lamps in East Grinstead existed right up until the early 1920s, after which the streets were lit by electricity. There were occasional cast-iron road direction signs, and telegraph poles had appeared in London Road by 1904, but were removed long ago. Some shops displayed overhanging trade signs, but there were no free-standing boards obstructing the walkways such as we now see. Today there is far too much street furniture in East Grinstead, and most of it is without merit.

One advantage of knowing the year date of every pre-1940 Frith photograph is that it can help postcard collectors date other companies' cards too. For example, in some views St Swithun's church tower displays a tall flagpole; thanks to Frith we can see that this pole had appeared by 1914 and vanished by 1931.

However, the dates of Frith's post-1940 views are known only approximately, and it has been a challenge to try to date them to within a year or two of when they were actually taken. This has been achieved usually by identifying car registration numbers when they are visible. However, in one case a cinema poster has been used, for it is easy to research which year the advertised film came out. One picture that the publishers had provisionally dated to around the year 1955 (E8020 - High Street and Tooth's shop) has been re-dated c1948 because a postcard of this scene exists postmarked July 1949. Having dated one picture accurately, it is simple to date others, particularly when they are part of a single batch - it is usually easy to see when certain photographs have all been taken on a particular day.

In this book the photographs are arranged as far as possible geographically, as though we are accompanying the photographer on a walking tour of the town, yet jumping back and forth in time between 1890 and 1965. On arrival by train at East Grinstead station we are first given a distant view of the town. We then move to the west end of the High Street, travelling east, taking in some of the side roads on the way. From Chequer Mead we go back to the junction of High Street and London Road, and continue north-west to Felbridge, again taking in some of the side roads on the way. Finally, we take a brief look at Dunnings, Saint Hill Green, Forest Row and Hartfield before returning (presumably by horse cab) to East Grinstead Station.

For those who would like to know more about the town and its ancient parish M J Leppard's recent book, 'A History of East Grinstead', is strongly recommended.

A Tour of the Town

General View 1890 27653
Looking east from a footpath that was later replaced by Brooklands Way, we see Queen's Road Cemetery and its two chapels on the right; the houses in Queen's Road itself; and on the skyline the tower of St Swithun's parish church. On the extreme left is part of the Union Workhouse, which was in Glen Vue Road (later Railway Approach).

High Street 1895
35223

In 1893, Constitutional
Buildings were opened
on the site of West
Buildings, and two shops
seen in the centre of the
previous picture have
made way for the Capital
& Counties Bank. To its
right, other shop fronts
have been rebuilt.
Among the group
outside the post office is
a well-wrapped
gentleman in a bath-
chair.

High Street 1890 27655

Three young men enjoy a chat in an almost deserted street. On the left is the post office, run by Fred Maplesden, who was also printer and publisher of the East Grinstead Household Almanack. At the end of Middle Row stands the house and shop (1877) of George Bailye, tailor and hairdresser. On the right is part of West Buildings - demolished in 1891 - with a hand lettered board advertising George Woolgar's iron works in nearby West Street.

High Street 1910 62800

There are plenty of horse-drawn carts in this view looking east. Maplesden is still running his printing works at No 1 - although it is no longer a post office - and at No 5 Gatland Bros. Stationers shop has a fine display of picture postcards including no doubt some Friths. Bailye the tailor has handed over the business to his relative Alec Johnson at No 1 Middle Row.

High Street 1921 70616

At No 11 next door to the Capital & Counties Bank (which later became the National Provincial Bank), is the hardware store of Miss Edith Annie Miller. Another bank, the London Joint City & Midland, has taken over the premises of Johnson the tailor, who moved to No 14 High Street.

High Street 1923
73350
Heavy motor traffic, a couple of carts, and a drover walking sheep along the street make this a lively scene. The two boy cyclists have been identified as Ken Brealey and Peter Chapman, both town residents. A war memorial, dedicated in 1922, has appeared on the south side of the street.

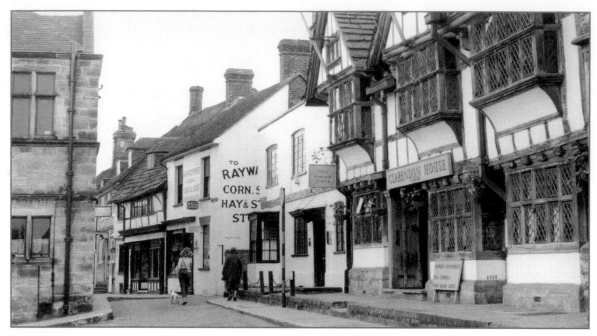

Clarendon House c1961 E8064
Moving back, we now see part of Constitutional Buildings on the left, Raywards corn and seed merchants at No 2 High Street, and the Clarendon House Restaurant, which closed in 1968. Clarendon House itself dates from c1500 and was once an inn called 'The George'.

High Street 1923 73353
A closer look at the war memorial, which on 23 July 1922 was unveiled by Admiral Sir Charles Madden of Herontye and dedicated by the vicar of East Grinstead, the Revd. Wilfrid Wadham Youard.

High Street 1933 85523

The memorial has now been fenced off, but about 1940 the railings were removed during a scrap metal drive and have never been replaced. The row of shops rebuilt in the 1890s has been replaced by Barclays Bank at Nos 19 - 23, and the Capital & Counties Bank displays its new name the National Provincial.

◀ **High Street 1965**
E8117
By the mid-1960s motor traffic through the town had increased considerably but London Transport's local bus services were still good, and the nearest stop lists four routes. At No 15, between the two banks, professional photographer Malcolm Powell was in business from 1959 to 1996.

▼ **High Street 1890** 27657
A closer look at Bailye's haircutting and shampooing rooms, No 1 Middle Row. At No 22 High Street is John Tooth, plumber and decorator, with his display board reading 'Registered Plumber - Agent to Le Grand and Sutcliff, Artesian Well Engineers'. John's sons Frederick and Edwin ran the stationers and drapers next door. On the right is the Jubilee Drinking Fountain, new in 1887.

▼ **High Street 1921** 70617
The imposing bulk of Nos 1-3 Middle Row, with its lower floor adapted as the new premises of the London Joint City and Midland Bank. The building still houses a bank but it is no longer called the Midland. We get a glimpse of the Crown Hotel (left) and some of the old shops in Middle Row.

▲ **Tooth's Shop 1927**
79594
On display are some children's books including A Nursery Alphabet, Animal Friends, A Merry Heart and Neddy; art materials; stationery; and a fine range of local view cards, all Frith's. Recognisable are the High Street, Sackville College, the Dorset Arms and Brambletye Castle.

◄ **High Street 1921** 70619
Edwin Tooth's stationers
shop, the 15th century
Tudor House at Nos 22 -
24. It sold also books and
art materials. Next door is
John Brook Allwork, wine
and spirit dealer, with open
cellar doors for deliveries in
front of his shop.

High Street 1923 73352
Horses and motor cars are happily co-existing in this scene looking
south-west. Henry Stephen Martin, chemists and Opthalmic
Opticians, opened at Nos 30 - 32 in the 1880s but sold the
business to E T Neathercoat, who kept the name 'H S Martin',
in 1921. The building was pulled down in 1968.

High Street 1928 81482

This brick pavement, which is higher than the street, is a favourite place for promenading. By 1927 Tyler & Co, Wine Merchants, had taken over the business of John Brook Allwork at Nos 26 - 28 The lime trees, which add so much to the charm of the street, were planted in 1874.

High Street c1948 E8015

In July 1943 the town received attention from the Luftwaffe, but the only building to be destroyed in the High Street was Brooker Bros premises, still not replaced when this picture was made. This firm of builders and contractors had the memorable telephone number East Grinstead 2.

◀ **High Street c1961** E8061
Looking west we see the junction of the High Street with West Street (left) and London Road (right), as well as Constitutional Buildings, by now adapted from clubrooms to shops and offices. P J May, Auctioneers, Surveyors and Estate Agents, are at No 2 London Road in premises shortly to be demolished, and part of the Swan Inn - closed 1963 and pulled down - is visible to their right.

High Street c1948

E8020

The Tudor House, with its magnificent stone slated roof, had a narrow escape from bombing in 1943. Dominating the picture is a 1937 saloon, registered at Coventry, and (presumably) its peak-capped chauffeur.

▼ High Street 1965 E8118

Even at this time it was difficult to find a parking space here. The van was registered in East Sussex in 1962. Since the previous picture was taken the Swan has been replace by new shops (1963) and P J May has new premises (1965).

◄ High Street c1962

E8090

In this unusual view looking south-west, taken apparently from an upper window of the Crown Hotel, we see the ever present line of parked cars, the newest of which, 6503MC, was registered in Middlesex in 1961. More seats have appeared on the brick pavement since the 1940s.

Old Houses c1957 E8051
This part of the High Street is generally known as 'behind Middle Row' and we are looking east towards the white painted Dorset Arms. At No 42 is a restaurant, Ye Olde Welcome, and next to it No 44 Lilian Styles, Fruiterer. A former athlete, she ran this shop from 1928 to 1981 and, it is said, sold fruit that was not always as fresh as it should have been.

High Street 1904 52900
The east end of the High Street, looking east. Ye Dorset Arms, once the town's principal coaching inn, had many changes of proprietor at this time, and its brickwork had already suffered the indignity of white paint. The handsome Dorset House next door is dated 1705. The motor car has one of the earliest registration plates (London, 1904) and may have been one of the first seen in East Grinstead.

Portland Road 1914 66758

This road was laid out in the early 1890s, its entry into the High Street necessitating the demolition of two lovely old cottages. We see the backs of three buildings in Middle Row; in the 1930s many people would gladly have seen them swept away too in order to make a wide High Street. Soaring above it all is the tower of St Swithun's parish church, with flagpole.

Hermitage Lane 1904
52907
This lane, which emerges on to the High Street immediately east of Portland Road, is much older and notable for its precipitous sandstone banks, which seem to be the source of admiration for an old gentleman - actually the photographer's assistant. The lane was named after a large house on it called The Hermitage, which no longer exists.

◄ Middle Row c1962

E8085

Only a small part of Middle Row is seen here: No 12 at the east end, with Normans (Outfitters and Camping Equipment) occupying Mann's old premises. In the centre is Dorset House, now taken over by the Dorset Arms for extra accommodation.

◀ **Ye Dorset Arms Hotel 1914** 66748
Mrs White was the proprietor of this hotel from 1911 to 1914. Between the entries of Hermitage Lane and Portland Road can just be seen the little shop of Arthur Paine, hairdresser; and on the right, at No 12 Middle Row, is William John Simmons Mann, Clothier and Hatter, established in 1887. He is advertising 'New Season's Goods.'

▼ **The Parish Church 1890** 27662
Dedicated to St Swithun, a Bishop of Winchester from 852 to 862, this imposing structure, dating from the 1790s, stands on the site of an earlier church that had been reduced to ruins by the collapse of its tower. It is in the Perpendicular style and was designed by James Wyatt. The vicar at the time of this picture was the Revd Douglas Yeoman Blakiston, who had trained as an artist. Almost the only change to the structure since 1890 has been the removal of the ivy.

◀ **High Street c1957**
E8053
This scene cannot be much later than 1957 as the still new-looking car (centre) was registered in 1956. From right to left are seen the Dorset Arms, Dorset House, Amherst House, Sackville House, a butcher's shop, and Cromwell House, with its tall chimneys.

High Street, Old Houses c1957 E8046
We have moved a short way east and get a closer view of Amherst House (c1340), Sackville House and the butcher's shop - whose proprietor was Mabel Harman. It is no longer a shop. The streamlined motor car was registered in 1949 and presumably belonged to the owner of Amherst House, outside which it is parked.

High Street 1904 52899
On the left, outside the butcher's at Nos 74 - 76, is probably the proprietor Frederick Rogers; on the right, outside No 65 - Miss Fanny Bodle, greengrocer, fruiterer, coal and wool dealer - are the shop staff. Sackville House (extreme left) has yet to have its timber framing revealed; it still has a covering of plasterwork.

High Street 1904 52901

Still looking west we see the impressive Cromwell House (1599) and, next to it, 'Ye Olde Easte Greenstede Café' run by William Stockdale. Across the street stands the Rose and Crown beerhouse whose licensee, Leonard George Gasson, ran it from 1900 to 1948. Francis Moore Wilcox had his saddlers shop at No 73 although by 1901 he no longer lived over the shop.

High Street 1921 70618

In the 17 years since the previous picture there has been almost no change. The Rose and Crown brewers Nalder & Collyer have had their sign re-lettered, but the Greenstede Café is still at No 82 and the shop between Cromwell House and Sackville House is still a butcher's, Ernest Octavius ('Ocky') Wood having succeeded Frederick Rogers in 1909.

Cromwell House 1923 73355
Of all High Street's timber-framed houses this one is the grandest. It was built in 1599 for Edward Payne, an ironworker, though by 1923 its resident was Robin Reid. It suffered a disastrous fire in December 1928 but was skilfully rebuilt the following year.

Picturesque Houses in the High Street 1933 85572
Prominent on the left is Sackville House, whose fabric for the most part is 15th century. Its
timber framing, previously hidden by plasterwork, was exposed in 1919. Until 1954 Geoffrey
Fuller Webb, a stained-glass window artist, lived here. The other 'picturesque' house (centre) is
Amherst House, the eastern part of which is 14th-century.

◄ **Sackville College
The Quad 1910** 62806
This Almshouse was
endowed in 1616 and
named after its founder
Robert Sackville, Earl of
Dorset. Here it is almost
submerged in ivy (since
removed). A wellhead is
just discernible at the
left, and to the right is
the chapel. The belfry is
a 19th century addition.
The College warden in
1910 was Frank Hill.

High Street c1955 E8044
Comparison with the picture, on page 39, will show the changes made to Cromwell House in its restoration of 1929. The left-hand ground-floor window now matches its fellow, three dormers have replaced the original two, the end elevation has plasterwork instead of tile-hanging, a larger window and more substantial bargeboards. On the right the rebuilt Rose and Crown (1938) is glimpsed behind a London Transport bus stop.

▼ **Lewes Road 1907** 57947
This is the continuation eastwards of High Street and we are looking west. The post-and-rail fencing, such a distinctive feature of this road, disappeared only recently. Cattle being driven to market are no longer seen, and the grand Victorian house, named Rocklands, also belongs to the past.

◄ **The Council Schools 1911** 63088
The first part to be opened, in 1861, was that on the right, and the rest was added in the 1870s and 1882. Later all the decorative work - finials, dormers, chimneys and belfry - was removed, leaving a much plainer facade, but the school survived until 1990, afterwards being adapted as Chequer Mead Arts Centre. Here some school children - including girls in pinafores (then the normal garb) - pose on the playing field.

College Lane 1907 57941
Named after Sackville College, this lane heads north off the east
end of the High Street, and we are looking north towards Blackwell
Hollow. The weatherboarded cottage with its unusual horizontally-
sliding windows and the group of four terraces at the far end all
came down in 1957/8, but Cima Cottage in the centre still stands,
now called Hill Cottage. The camera of 'Mr Frith' has as usual
attracted the attention of several local children.

The Top of Blackwell Hollow 1907 57948
Looking north from College Lane where it leads into Blackwell
Hollow we see on the left the entrance to a large house called
Stoneleigh and, behind the cyclist, the entrance to East Court -
then a private residence but latterly adapted as council offices.
Estcots Drive now comes in on the right and most of the trees
are gone.

London Road 1891
29587
Whilst changes to the High Street have been few, London Road - here seen from the corner of the High Street - looked very different 110 years ago. On the left is the Swan Inn; next to it a saddler's shop (George Brinkhurst). On the right is Head's Bank, which failed in 1892 and was taken over by Lloyd's Bank (still there). Beyond, Albion Russell's boot and shoe shop, which is still functioning as Russell & Bromley.

◀ **London Road 1907**
57934
Three years later Joseph Blakeman has his name displayed on The Swan: he was licensee from 1907 - 1910. Although there were many shops in this road few people are visible in this scene, though a cart turning into the High Street brings it to life.

◀ **London Road 1904** 52904
The Southdown & East Grinstead Breweries Ltd, owners of The Swan, have now smartened it up and rebuilt the lower floor completely. George Underwood has his name painted on a large board in the centre, but he was licensee only during 1904/05. Beyond Brinkhurst's shop is a glimpse of Armstrong's, a wine and spirit business that has functioned in the same building from c1890 to the present day.

◀ **London Road 1914**
66749
In that last glorious summer before the Great War, the town is looking a little more lively, with some early motor cars visible. The pavement outside The Swan has been lowered and the steps altered. Licensees changed frequently at this inn, and it is T Izard who now has his name displayed, keeping a signwriter in work if nothing else.

London Road 1914

66750

A superb composition, looking north-west. At No 16, E Dutt, cycle agent and gramophone dealer; at No 18, L Raven who had this newsagents and stationers business for only a short time; and next to that, the newly opened Cinema de Luxe, which despite its name was a very small and badly ventilated picture house that had once been the town's public hall.

London Road c1955 E8034

In the centre are new shops and flats that replaced Nos 23 - 43, all of which were bombed in 1943 and 1944. The spire of the former Wesleyan church (1881) is visible. On the left the Swan Hotel is still intact but now owned by Tamplins. Next to it, shops built in the 1930s have replaced the old saddlers and bootmakers at Nos 8 and 10. There are far more people about than in earlier views and a pedestrian or 'zebra' crossing has now become necessary.

London Road c1961 E8060

A good view of Gamley's toyshop, which opened in its new building in 1937: 'For the finest and largest selection of toys in the town visit our splendid show room upstairs.' Armstrong's wine merchants at No 12, one of the oldest surviving buildings in the road, now has a new upper window on its south side.

London Road c1959 E8057
Moving down we get a closer look at the 1951 and 1952-built neo-Georgian shops and flats on the east side, including some well-known multi-national stores: John Collier, Dolcis, W H Smith and J Sainsbury. The odd looking structure against the sky is a concrete water tower, erected in 1913.

London Road c1959 E8058
Another well-known multi-national dominates this view; the branch has been here since about 1930, though the left-hand extension is a post-War development on the site of the Cinema de Luxe, which burned down in 1940; it had been renamed the Solarius in 1934.

▼ London Road c1961 E8059

Moving down a short way we see on the left a shop that had stood empty since 1940; it was often mentioned in the local press. Not until 1967 was it demolished and its site is now the entry to Queen's Walk. Beyond are Timothy Whites, chemist; Bobbies Café; Dewhurst, butcher; Raymonde, ladies' fashion; and King's motor garage. All are gone.

▼ London Road c1960 E8066

The poster on the left in the derelict shop is advertising a football match on Saturday, October 1st, which would make the year 1960. All the motorists have considerately parked their cars on the same side of the road, leaving plenty of room for through traffic - if only they would do so nowadays! The narrow left-hand pavement was considerably widened in 1982, the road in consequence being narrowed here.

▲ London Road 1965

E8116

An animated scene with plenty of walkers, including one man who has just cracked his head on an overhanging shop blind courtesy of Bata Shoes. The cinema poster on the wall of Newsagents & Stationers Supply Ltd (the same building that Raven had in 1914) advertises The Hill, a British prison drama starring Sean Connery and released in 1965.

◀ **London Road c1961** E8069
Our photographer has now moved down a little further and turned round to look up the road, facing south. The old Wesleyan church went in the late 1950s to be replaced by Fine Fare Supermarket (Nos 19 - 21) and Currys radio and TV shop (No 17) with flats above.

◀ **London Road 1965**
E8101
We are again looking south by Ernest Tyrrell's butchers shop, with Flinns the cleaners next door at No 42, and beyond the next shop is the entrance to King's Garages. All these went in the 1970s and Forbuoys and Boots now occupy their site.

◄ London Road 1965

E8112

A bustling and lively shopping street but not yet choked with motor traffic. Tyrell's butchers shop at No 44 is a reminder that the town then had several such shops and now, in the whole of the town centre, there is not one left.

▼ London Road 1890 27659

Looking south-east on a now unrecognisable scene. On the left is the Literary and Scientific Institute (1888-1937), next to which are three old cottages called Rock Gardens. Beyond them is the Grosvenor Hall and George Bridgland, china, glass and piano dealer. The Whitehall now stands on their site. On the right are Elm Cottages, of which four were later altered to shops and one pulled down to make way for a new post office (1896).

◄ London Road 1904 52903

From the south-east, a look at the Institute, which has now sprouted a clock, put up in 1891 in memory of Thomas Cramp, the town's diarist and total abstainer. On the left are the offices of the East Grinstead Observer, at that time owned by Farncombe & Co, printers and lithographers. Beyond are the four little cottages now adapted into three shops (one of which, Ada Francis, is advertising her Dining & Tea Rooms), and the post office, which replaced that at Maplesden's shop in the High Street in 1896.

London Road 1904
52902
The Grosvenor Hall has now been rebuilt with an extra storey, complete with dormer windows, and George Bridgland's sign advertises 'Pianos for Sale and Hire'. Across the road two smart new shops reflect the town's increasing prosperity: No 48 Marcus Walker, shoemaker and repairer; and No 48a Frank Blanchard, draper. Further up, some workmen appear to be laying the pavement.

London Road 1910
62801
By 1907 the caterers
Letheby and
Christopher had taken
over the Grosvenor Hall
and altered it to include
a restaurant, with a
grand Edwardian style
glazed canopy across
the pavement. An early
motor car avoids
running down several
pedestrians walking in
the road.

◄ **London Road 1921**
70620
Cinemas became known as picture palaces, so the wording has been changed since 1914. Three new shops, built c1915, have appeared on the right: Wilmer, tobacconist; Joyce Turner, baby linen; and Ashby, china dealer. A branch of Sainsbury's (centre) opened in 1921.

◀ **London Road 1914** 66751
In November 1910 Letheby & Christopher further adapted the hall as a theatre and cinema, renaming it the Whitehall, hence the large - indeed intrusive - illuminated sign. The Grosvenor Restaurant was retained. On the opposite side some trees have made way for rather poor-looking shops and two rival motor garages - the North Sussex and King's.

▼ **London Road 1965** E8106
Prominent is the Whitehall (1936), which stands on the site of Rock Gardens and the Grosvenor Hall, and shops that replaced the Jubilee Institute (1938). Left to right: Murrells, drapers; Batemans, opticians; International Stores, grocers; Freeman, Hardy & Willis, shoes; Kerry, ladies' fashions; and Lovibonds, wine merchants. The Rolling Stones once performed at the Whitehall.

◀ **London Road 1965** E8114
Only two of the small shops - the nearer of which is Arthur S Fry, family butcher - now survive from the four converted from cottages in the 1890s; the other two were demolished in July 1965, not long before this picture was made. The traffic signals at the Queen's Road/King Street junction were installed in 1954. Plenty of people are doing their morning shopping here before supermarkets became universal.

London Road 1965 E8113
The type of double-deck bus seen in the distance was introduced on the Reigate - East Grinstead service on 15th September 1965. The van belonging to Caffyns Ltd is not far from home as their motor garage is just round the corner in King Street. Adding greatly to this intriguing scene is the lady with black horses on her dress.

▶ **The Cottage Hospital 1911** 63090
If this building in Queen's Road does not look much like a hospital that is because, originally, it was not. When built in 1879 it was a coffee tavern, which soon failed; in 1885 it became a holiday home, but in 1902 was adapted as a hospital, functioning as such until 1936. It was demolished in c1986. Looking south-west, we have a glimpse of some of the road's working-class housing.

King Street 1937 87786
Laid out in 1934/5, it was named after Harry King of King's
Garages, London Road. Both the Radio Centre cinema and Caffyns
Garage date from 1936; the garage survives minus its cream tiles
but the cinema was closed in 1989, its glorious 1930s opulence
having faded by then. Its rather unusual name was inspired by the
Radio City Theatre in New York.

London Road 1910
62802
Moving north-west and turning round to face south-east we see on the left three new shops where formerly stood trees: Home & Colonial Tea Stores, John Humphrey, fishmonger and William Tomlinson, stationer, all opened in 1909. On the right Charles Morton Wilson, draper, is advertising a 'Great Sale'. Rock Gardens and the Grosvenor Hall are glimpsed in the background.

◀ **London Road c1959** E805
This view looking south-east
shows how much the town's
character had changed
since the 1890s. The shops
on the left date from the
1930s; the mock Tudor
Brighton Co-operative store
was opened in 1931. Its tin
milk-float stands outside.
The concrete bus shelter
and bus stop were
dispensed with in c1977
when all buses were re-
routed down Railway
Approach.

London Road 1923 73357

These magnificent elms, which belonged to the Placelands Estate, were all removed in 1925 to make way for yet more shops. The Railway Hotel (right) dated from 1856 and was owned by brewers Nalder & Collyer. Beneath its name board was the badge of the Cyclists Touring Club. Dixons the Chemist is seen on the corner of Railway Approach.

The Glanfield Hotel c1961 E8070

Unusually named after its architect, it replaced the Railway Hotel in 1938. In recent years it was renamed the Broadway and its appearance ruined by cement rendering and painted brickwork. We have just a glimpse of Railway Approach before many of its small houses were demolished in about 1963.

St James's Road 1907 57946

Linking London Road and Station Road, it was laid out in 1890/1; this view is looking east to London Road. All the houses on the right were demolished in the 1970s for offices, this spoiling what had been a handsome crescent. The terrace on the left was spared. Next to it is the Masonic Hall (1898).

London Road 1904
52906
Half a mile from the town centre and looking north-west we see a small parade of shops, with the Church of Our Lady and St Peter (1898) behind. The house to the left of the shops was inhabited by Walter Wells, a gardener, and his wife Frances, who took in laundry. Many people in the 1900s earned their living in this way.

Moat Road and Moat Church 1891 29588
One of the earliest views of this Congregational (later United Reformed) church, erected in 1870 by the Nonconformist local builder Edward Steer, who also built the cottage on the corner. From here his son, also named Edward, published a local newspaper, The Southern Free Press, until 1891.

London Road 1904 52905
Moat Church and the little row of shops are the main points of interest in this view looking south-east, the road itself being almost deserted. The sidewalks are paved in brick, a luxury they do not enjoy today. The businesses are: C Camfield, hardware; and Charles Sheather, Brockhurst Dairy.

Moat Road 1907 57942
This purely residential and rather select road only later became part of the main route to Tunbridge Wells. Left is Moat House (c1866), the home of Edward Whitley Hughes, a Welsh solicitor and part-time clerk to the Urban District Council for many years. Delivery boys pose for 'Mr Frith' and his camera.

St Michael's School 1923 73358
Standing on the north-west side of Moat Road, this was an Anglican school for girls, run by St Margaret's Convent. The building on the right was formerly a private house, Oakfield Lodge, built by Edward Steer. About 1918 an extension (centre) was made to join the former St Margaret's College (left background). Since closure in 1976 much of it has gone but part survives as Neale House. This view is looking south-west.

▼ **Convent Courtyard 1890** 27673
This view from the quadrangle is looking east. At the time of this photograph the
Convent's first Mother Superior, Sister Alice (Crocker), was still in charge; she died
in 1902 aged 72 and her replacement was Sister Erminild, a daughter of J M Neale,
the founder.

▼ **St Margaret's Convent 1909** 61961
From the quadrangle looking north-west, we see the cross erected in memory of
Sister Amy, who in 1857 contracted scarlet fever while out nursing. The Convent
had the services of a Chaplain, the Reverend Reginald Ernest Hutton, and
employed a full-time gardener who lived in a cottage on the premises.

▲ **St Margaret's Convent
1909** 61948
The Society of St
Margaret, an Anglican
sisterhood founded by
the Reverend John
Mason Neale in 1855,
took up residence here
from 1870, four years
after their founder's
death. This is the north-
west front looking east
and showing the chapel
and its tower (1883).

◀ **St Margaret's Convent 1909**
61962

The camera has been swung round slightly and we are now looking west, with part of the chapel seen on the left. In 1975 the Sisters moved into new premises and sold off the whole of the Convent buildings, which have been adapted into high-quality flats.

◀ **The Queen Victoria Hospital 1935** 87154
This purpose-built hospital, which replaced the one in Queen's Road, was built in Holtye Road and opened in January 1936. If this picture is correctly dated it must have been taken very shortly before opening, possibly in December. The hospital was paid for by public subscription; Sir Robert Kindersley, a banker, gave land for its construction and one of the wards was named after him.

Mount Noddy 1928 81486
No one is certain about the origin of this strange name, except that it has nothing to do with Enid Blyton. The Urban District Council laid out the field as a recreation ground and children's play area in 1914. The boy on the swing is Norman Pearson, watched by his mother; Norman still runs a cycle shop in the High Street. Mount Noddy Cottage, nestling in the trees, was demolished in the 1950s.

London Road 1925 77149
Continuing north-west towards Felbridge from the Moat Road junction we see the Italianate Church of Our Lady and St Peter, looking south east. The motor vehicle, on the right, belonged to Martin Simmons, fishmonger. The ivy-clad house, named the Hollies, would be replaced by more shops in 1928.

The Queen Victoria Hospital c1962 E8089
The hospital has had many additions over the years but the original building facing Holtye Road is little changed. A short extension to the left, the children's Pea-Nut Ward, was opened by Queen Elizabeth the Queen Mother in July 1955.

London Road 1914

66752

Looking south-east we see, on the left beyond the railway bridge, the Gas & Water Co. showroom - on whose site is now the entry to 'Focus'. Of the fine villas on the right dating from c1888 only the tall twin-gabled one survives, adapted as Rentokil House. In 1914, it was the shop and home of William Taylor, furniture dealer.

Felbridge

Felbridge, The Church 1910 62811
The village lies two miles north-west of East Grinstead town centre, most of it being in Surrey. St John the Divine dates from 1865, a local landowner, Charles Henry Gatty, having overseen its construction. Designed by William White it is built of rubble stone in the decorated style. The headstone commemorates 'Blanche, the beloved wife of Evelyn Borrer Blaker, who died 22nd March 1908'. Four years later the widower himself died.

Felbridge, The Village 1925 77153
Looking north at the junction of the Crawley and Godstone roads we see the Star Inn, a much re-built 17th-century timber framed house, although little altered since the 19th century. The Felbridge Garage was converted from a smithy. An open top bus is heading for Lingfield, Godstone, Caterham and Croydon.

Felbridge, The Village 1928 81488
Three years later the Star, with S J Clee's name over the doorway, is unchanged, although a forecourt for the use of motorists has been added; but the Felbridge Garage now has a tea shop, with new windows.

Felbridge, The Village 1965 F15011
Little change to the Star but its car park has been extended, and a new restaurant has appeared - since demolished and replaced by an even bigger eatery. The garage's tea shop has been gutted and altered to a car showroom. There is a great increase in street furniture such as lamp posts, flagpoles and traffic islands, whose black and white paintwork is a hangover from wartime blackout conditions.

Dunnings Mill and Saint Hill Green

Dunnings Mill 1907 57950
Imagine the delight of the Frith photographer on encountering this charming scene three-quarters of a mile south of the town centre, just off Dunnings Road. Dunnings Mill has been converted into a restaurant, but the pond was long ago filled in.

Saint Hill Green 1907
57952
This hamlet is one-and-a-half miles south of the town centre and we are looking east, with the road to Dunnings and East Grinstead leading off left and that to Tyes Cross to the right. Many children from the nearby school have foregathered to have their photograph taken; how could they resist?

Forest Row

Forest Row, The Village 1903 48265
Looking north at the junction of the roads from
Lewes and Tunbridge Wells, we see yet another
group of children and an unattended horse-drawn
cart. On the left is Holy Trinity Church (designed by
William Moseley, 1836) and in the centre, the village
hall (1892) designed by J M Brydon and erected by
Job Luxford, a local builder.

Forest Row, The Village 1931 83750
Several members of the Martin family had businesses in the village. C Martin ran a motor garage (next to Lloyds Bank, left) while across the street Bernard and George Martin had a drapery store, displaying their name on the end wall; Henry Martin ran tea-rooms and Miss Nellie Martin was a stationer. The open tourer was registered in Surrey in 1926.

◀ **Hartfield, The Village 1906** 56692
A knife sharpener is at work just outside the Dorset Arms Hotel in this view looking south-west. Stephen Bentley, wine and spirit merchant and farmer, advertised 'good stabling, lock-up coach houses' at the inn, whose appearance is little changed today, though the name was altered to 'The Hay Waggon' some years ago. John Killick, grocer's and draper's shop, was in business from c1886 to c1922 and was also registrar of births and deaths.

Hartfield

◀ **Hartfield
High Street 1906** 56693
This view, also looking
south-west, shows Vine
House on the right, with
its little shop and post
office run by Fanny
Medhurst, stationer and
sub postmistress. The
whole row was built
between the 14th and
16th centuries. Latterly,
the sloping end has been
sliced off, and the shop
closed in about 1967.

◀**East Grinstead
Railway Station 1911**
63087
It is now time to leave
the town and what better
way than by train? This
station, the town's third,
was opened in 1882 and
included accommodation
for the stationmaster,
who in 1911 was William
Langley. The whole
building came down in
1971, to be replaced by
the present prefabricated
structure.

The Railway Viaduct, Bellaggio 1890 27669
Shortly after leaving East Grinstead by train we cross the
magnificent Cooks Pond Viaduct, with its fine view. 'Bellaggio' was
the name of the estate later known as Dormans Park. The viaduct is
65 ft high and about 650 ft long, and was opened in 1884.

Index

Blackwell Hollow 43

College Lane 42

Cottage Hospital 62

Council Schools 41

Cromwell House 39

Glanfield Hotel 67

Hermitage Lane 32-33

High Street 18-19, 20-21, 22, 23,
   24-25, 26, 27, 28-29, 30, 35, 36,
   37, 38, 40-41

King Street 63

Lewes Road 41

London Road 44-45, 46-47, 48-49,
   50, 51, 52-53, 54-55, 56-57, 58-59,
   60-61, 62, 64-65, 66-67, 68-69, 70,
   75, 76-77

Middle Row 34

Moat Church 70

Moat Road 70, 71

Mount Noddy 74-75

Parish Church 35

Portland Road 31

Queen Victoria Hospital 74, 75

Railway Station 87

St James's Road 67

St Margaret's Convent 72-73

St Michael's School 71

Sackville College 40

Tooth's Shop 24-25

Ye Dorset Arms Hotel 34-35

Around East Grinstead

Bellaggio Railway Viaduct 88

Dunnings Mill 80-81

Felbridge 78, 79

Forest Row 82-83, 84-85

Hartfield 86-87

Saint Hill Green 80-81

Frith Book Co Titles

www.francisfrith.co.uk

The Frith Book Company publishes over 100 new titles each year. A selection of those currently available are listed below. For latest catalogue please contact Frith Book Co.

Town Books 96 pages, approx 100 photos. County and Themed Books 128 pages, approx 150 photos (unless specified). All titles hardback laminated case and jacket except those indicated pb (paperback)

Amersham, Chesham & Rickmansworth (pb)			Derby (pb)	1-85937-367-4	£9.99
	1-85937-340-2	£9.99	Derbyshire (pb)	1-85937-196-5	£9.99
Ancient Monuments & Stone Circles	1-85937-143-4	£17.99	Devon (pb)	1-85937-297-x	£9.99
Aylesbury (pb)	1-85937-227-9	£9.99	Dorset (pb)	1-85937-269-4	£9.99
Bakewell	1-85937-113-2	£12.99	Dorset Churches	1-85937-172-8	£17.99
Barnstaple (pb)	1-85937-300-3	£9.99	Dorset Coast (pb)	1-85937-299-6	£9.99
Bath (pb)	1-85937419-0	£9.99	Dorset Living Memories	1-85937-210-4	£14.99
Bedford (pb)	1-85937-205-8	£9.99	Down the Severn	1-85937-118-3	£14.99
Berkshire (pb)	1-85937-191-4	£9.99	Down the Thames (pb)	1-85937-278-3	£9.99
Berkshire Churches	1-85937-170-1	£17.99	Down the Trent	1-85937-311-9	£14.99
Blackpool (pb)	1-85937-382-8	£9.99	Dublin (pb)	1-85937-231-7	£9.99
Bognor Regis (pb)	1-85937-431-x	£9.99	East Anglia (pb)	1-85937-265-1	£9.99
Bournemouth	1-85937-067-5	£12.99	East London	1-85937-080-2	£14.99
Bradford (pb)	1-85937-204-x	£9.99	East Sussex	1-85937-130-2	£14.99
Brighton & Hove(pb)	1-85937-192-2	£8.99	Eastbourne	1-85937-061-6	£12.99
Bristol (pb)	1-85937-264-3	£9.99	Edinburgh (pb)	1-85937-193-0	£8.99
British Life A Century Ago (pb)	1-85937-213-9	£9.99	England in the 1880s	1-85937-331-3	£17.99
Buckinghamshire (pb)	1-85937-200-7	£9.99	English Castles (pb)	1-85937-434-4	£9.99
Camberley (pb)	1-85937-222-8	£9.99	English Country Houses	1-85937-161-2	£17.99
Cambridge (pb)	1-85937-422-0	£9.99	Essex (pb)	1-85937-270-8	£9.99
Cambridgeshire (pb)	1-85937-420-4	£9.99	Exeter	1-85937-126-4	£12.99
Canals & Waterways (pb)	1-85937-291-0	£9.99	Exmoor	1-85937-132-9	£14.99
Canterbury Cathedral (pb)	1-85937-179-5	£9.99	Falmouth	1-85937-066-7	£12.99
Cardiff (pb)	1-85937-093-4	£9.99	Folkestone (pb)	1-85937-124-8	£9.99
Carmarthenshire	1-85937-216-3	£14.99	Glasgow (pb)	1-85937-190-6	£9.99
Chelmsford (pb)	1-85937-310-0	£9.99	Gloucestershire	1-85937-102-7	£14.99
Cheltenham (pb)	1-85937-095-0	£9.99	Great Yarmouth (pb)	1-85937-426-3	£9.99
Cheshire (pb)	1-85937-271-6	£9.99	Greater Manchester (pb)	1-85937-266-x	£9.99
Chester	1-85937-090-x	£12.99	Guildford (pb)	1-85937-410-7	£9.99
Chesterfield	1-85937-378-x	£9.99	Hampshire (pb)	1-85937-279-1	£9.99
Chichester (pb)	1-85937-228-7	£9.99	Hampshire Churches (pb)	1-85937-207-4	£9.99
Colchester (pb)	1-85937-188-4	£8.99	Harrogate	1-85937-423-9	£9.99
Cornish Coast	1-85937-163-9	£14.99	Hastings & Bexhill (pb)	1-85937-131-0	£9.99
Cornwall (pb)	1-85937-229-5	£9.99	Heart of Lancashire (pb)	1-85937-197-3	£9.99
Cornwall Living Memories	1-85937-248-1	£14.99	Helston (pb)	1-85937-214-7	£9.99
Cotswolds (pb)	1-85937-230-9	£9.99	Hereford (pb)	1-85937-175-2	£9.99
Cotswolds Living Memories	1-85937-255-4	£14.99	Herefordshire	1-85937-174-4	£14.99
County Durham	1-85937-123-x	£14.99	Hertfordshire (pb)	1-85937-247-3	£9.99
Croydon Living Memories	1-85937-162-0	£9.99	Horsham (pb)	1-85937-432-8	£9.99
Cumbria	1-85937-101-9	£14.99	Humberside	1-85937-215-5	£14.99
Dartmoor	1-85937-145-0	£14.99	Hythe, Romney Marsh & Ashford	1-85937-256-2	£9.99

Available from your local bookshop or from the publisher

Frith Book Co Titles (continued)

Title	ISBN	Price	Title	ISBN	Price
Ipswich (pb)	1-85937-424-7	£9.99	St Ives (pb)	1-85937415-8	£9.99
Ireland (pb)	1-85937-181-7	£9.99	Scotland (pb)	1-85937-182-5	£9.99
Isle of Man (pb)	1-85937-268-6	£9.99	Scottish Castles (pb)	1-85937-323-2	£9.99
Isles of Scilly	1-85937-136-1	£14.99	Sevenoaks & Tunbridge	1-85937-057-8	£12.99
Isle of Wight (pb)	1-85937-429-8	£9.99	Sheffield, South Yorks (pb)	1-85937-267-8	£9.99
Isle of Wight Living Memories	1-85937-304-6	£14.99	Shrewsbury (pb)	1-85937-325-9	£9.99
Kent (pb)	1-85937-189-2	£9.99	Shropshire (pb)	1-85937-326-7	£9.99
Kent Living Memories	1-85937-125-6	£14.99	Somerset	1-85937-153-1	£14.99
Lake District (pb)	1-85937-275-9	£9.99	South Devon Coast	1-85937-107-8	£14.99
Lancaster, Morecambe & Heysham (pb)	1-85937-233-3	£9.99	South Devon Living Memories	1-85937-168-x	£14.99
Leeds (pb)	1-85937-202-3	£9.99	South Hams	1-85937-220-1	£14.99
Leicester	1-85937-073-x	£12.99	Southampton (pb)	1-85937-427-1	£9.99
Leicestershire (pb)	1-85937-185-x	£9.99	Southport (pb)	1-85937-425-5	£9.99
Lincolnshire (pb)	1-85937-433-6	£9.99	Staffordshire	1-85937-047-0	£12.99
Liverpool & Merseyside (pb)	1-85937-234-1	£9.99	Stratford upon Avon	1-85937-098-5	£12.99
London (pb)	1-85937-183-3	£9.99	Suffolk (pb)	1-85937-221-x	£9.99
Ludlow (pb)	1-85937-176-0	£9.99	Suffolk Coast	1-85937-259-7	£14.99
Luton (pb)	1-85937-235-x	£9.99	Surrey (pb)	1-85937-240-6	£9.99
Maidstone	1-85937-056-x	£14.99	Sussex (pb)	1-85937-184-1	£9.99
Manchester (pb)	1-85937-198-1	£9.99	Swansea (pb)	1-85937-167-1	£9.99
Middlesex	1-85937-158-2	£14.99	Tees Valley & Cleveland	1-85937-211-2	£14.99
New Forest	1-85937-128-0	£14.99	Thanet (pb)	1-85937-116-7	£9.99
Newark (pb)	1-85937-366-6	£9.99	Tiverton (pb)	1-85937-178-7	£9.99
Newport, Wales (pb)	1-85937-258-9	£9.99	Torbay	1-85937-063-2	£12.99
Newquay (pb)	1-85937-421-2	£9.99	Truro	1-85937-147-7	£12.99
Norfolk (pb)	1-85937-195-7	£9.99	Victorian and Edwardian Cornwall	1-85937-252-x	£14.99
Norfolk Living Memories	1-85937-217-1	£14.99	Victorian & Edwardian Devon	1-85937-253-8	£14.99
Northamptonshire	1-85937-150-7	£14.99	Victorian & Edwardian Kent	1-85937-149-3	£14.99
Northumberland Tyne & Wear (pb)	1-85937-281-3	£9.99	Vic & Ed Maritime Album	1-85937-144-2	£17.99
North Devon Coast	1-85937-146-9	£14.99	Victorian and Edwardian Sussex	1-85937-157-4	£14.99
North Devon Living Memories	1-85937-261-9	£14.99	Victorian & Edwardian Yorkshire	1-85937-154-x	£14.99
North London	1-85937-206-6	£14.99	Victorian Seaside	1-85937-159-0	£17.99
North Wales (pb)	1-85937-298-8	£9.99	Villages of Devon (pb)	1-85937-293-7	£9.99
North Yorkshire (pb)	1-85937-236-8	£9.99	Villages of Kent (pb)	1-85937-294-5	£9.99
Norwich (pb)	1-85937-194-9	£8.99	Villages of Sussex (pb)	1-85937-295-3	£9.99
Nottingham (pb)	1-85937-324-0	£9.99	Warwickshire (pb)	1-85937-203-1	£9.99
Nottinghamshire (pb)	1-85937-187-6	£9.99	Welsh Castles (pb)	1-85937-322-4	£9.99
Oxford (pb)	1-85937-411-5	£9.99	West Midlands (pb)	1-85937-289-9	£9.99
Oxfordshire (pb)	1-85937-430-1	£9.99	West Sussex	1-85937-148-5	£14.99
Peak District (pb)	1-85937-280-5	£9.99	West Yorkshire (pb)	1-85937-201-5	£9.99
Penzance	1-85937-069-1	£12.99	Weymouth (pb)	1-85937-209-0	£9.99
Peterborough (pb)	1-85937-219-8	£9.99	Wiltshire (pb)	1-85937-277-5	£9.99
Piers	1-85937-237-6	£17.99	Wiltshire Churches (pb)	1-85937-171-x	£9.99
Plymouth	1-85937-119-1	£12.99	Wiltshire Living Memories	1-85937-245-7	£14.99
Poole & Sandbanks (pb)	1-85937-251-1	£9.99	Winchester (pb)	1-85937-428-x	£9.99
Preston (pb)	1-85937-212-0	£9.99	Windmills & Watermills	1-85937-242-2	£17.99
Reading (pb)	1-85937-238-4	£9.99	Worcester (pb)	1-85937-165-5	£9.99
Romford (pb)	1-85937-319-4	£9.99	Worcestershire	1-85937-152-3	£14.99
Salisbury (pb)	1-85937-239-2	£9.99	York (pb)	1-85937-199-x	£9.99
Scarborough (pb)	1-85937-379-8	£9.99	Yorkshire (pb)	1-85937-186-8	£9.99
St Albans (pb)	1-85937-341-0	£9.99	Yorkshire Living Memories	1-85937-166-3	£14.99

See Frith books on the internet www.francisfrith.co.uk

FRITH PRODUCTS & SERVICES

Francis Frith would doubtless be pleased to know that the pioneering publishing venture he started in 1860 still continues today. A hundred and forty years later, The Francis Frith Collection continues in the same innovative tradition and is now one of the foremost publishers of vintage photographs in the world. Some of the current activities include:

Interior Decoration

Today Frith's photographs can be seen framed and as giant wall murals in thousands of pubs, restaurants, hotels, banks, retail stores and other public buildings throughout the country. In every case they enhance the unique local atmosphere of the places they depict and provide reminders of gentler days in an increasingly busy and frenetic world.

Product Promotions

Frith products are used by many major companies to promote the sales of their own products or to reinforce their own history and heritage. Frith promotions have been used by Hovis bread, Courage beers, Scots Porage Oats, Colman's mustard, Cadbury's foods, Mellow Birds coffee, Dunhill pipe tobacco, Guinness, and Bulmer's Cider.

Genealogy and Family History

As the interest in family history and roots grows world-wide, more and more people are turning to Frith's photographs of Great Britain for images of the towns, villages and streets where their ancestors lived; and, of course, photographs of the churches and chapels where their ancestors were christened, married and buried are an essential part of every genealogy tree and family album.

Frith Products

All Frith photographs are available Framed or just as Mounted Prints and Posters (size 23 x 16 inches). These may be ordered from the address below. From time to time other products - Address Books, Calendars, Table Mats, etc - are available.

The Internet

Already twenty thousand Frith photographs can be viewed and purchased on the internet through the Frith websites and a myriad of partner sites.

For more detailed information on Frith companies and products, look at these sites:

www.francisfrith.co.uk
www.francisfrith.com
(for North American visitors)

See the complete list of Frith Books at:

www.francisfrith.co.uk

This web site is regularly updated with the latest list of publications from the Frith Book Company. If you wish to buy books relating to another part of the country that your local bookshop does not stock, you may purchase on-line.

For further information, trade, or author enquiries please contact us at the address below:
The Francis Frith Collection, Frith's Barn, Teffont, Salisbury, Wiltshire, England SP3 5QP.
Tel: +44 (0)1722 716 376 Fax: +44 (0)1722 716 881 Email: sales@francisfrith.co.uk

See Frith books on the internet www.francisfrith.co.uk

TO RECEIVE YOUR FREE MOUNTED PRINT

Mounted Print
Overall size 14 x 11 inches

Cut out this Voucher and return it with your remittance for £2.25 to cover postage and handling, to UK addresses. For overseas addresses please include £4.00 post and handling. Choose any photograph included in this book. Your SEPIA print will be A4 in size, and mounted in a cream mount with burgundy rule line, overall size 14 x 11 inches.

Order additional Mounted Prints at HALF PRICE (only £7.49 each*)

If there are further pictures you would like to order, possibly as gifts for friends and family, purchase them at half price (no additional postage and handling required).

Have your Mounted Prints framed*

For an additional £14.95 per print you can have your chosen Mounted Print framed in an elegant polished wood and gilt moulding, overall size 16 x 13 inches (no additional postage and handling required).

---

* IMPORTANT!
These special prices are only available if ordered using the original voucher on this page (no copies permitted) and at the same time as your free Mounted Print, for delivery to the same address

---

Frith Collectors' Guild

From time to time we publish a magazine of news and stories about Frith photographs and further special offers of Frith products. If you would like 12 months FREE membership, please return this form.

Send completed forms to:
The Francis Frith Collection, Frith's Barn, Teffont, Salisbury, Wiltshire SP3 5QP

Voucher for **FREE** and Reduced Price Frith Prints

Picture no.	Page number	Qty	Mounted @ £7.49	Framed + £14.95	Total Cost
		1	**Free of charge***	£	£
			£7.49	£	£
			£7.49	£	£
			£7.49	£	£
			£7.49	£	£
			£7.49	£	£

Please allow 28 days for delivery   *** Post & handling**   **£2.25**

Book Title . . . .   **Total Order Cost**   **£**

Please do not photocopy this voucher. Only the original is valid, so please cut it out and return it to us.

I enclose a cheque / postal order for £ . . . .
made payable to 'The Francis Frith Collection'
OR please debit my Mastercard / Visa / Switch / Amex card
(credit cards please on all overseas orders)

Number . . . .

Issue No (Switch only) . . . . .Valid from (Amex/Switch) . . . .

Expires . . . . Signature . . . .

Name Mr/Mrs/Ms . . . .

Address . . . .

. . . .

. . . .

Postcode . . . . Daytime Tel No . . . .

Email Address . . . .

Valid to 31/12/04

The Francis Frith Collectors' Guild

Please enrol me as a member for 12 months free of charge.

Name Mr/Mrs/Ms . . . .

Address . . . .

. . . .

. . . .

. . . . Postcode . . . .

Would you like to find out more about Francis Frith?

We have recently recruited some entertaining speakers who are happy to visit local groups, clubs and societies to give an illustrated talk documenting Frith's travels and photographs. If you are a member of such a group and are interested in hosting a presentation, we would love to hear from you.

Our speakers bring with them a small selection of our local town and county books, together with sample prints. They are happy to take orders. A small proportion of the order value is donated to the group who have hosted the presentation. The talks are therefore an excellent way of fundraising for small groups and societies.

Can you help us with information about any of the Frith photographs in this book?

We are gradually compiling an historical record for each of the photographs in the Frith archive. It is always fascinating to find out the names of the people shown in the pictures, as well as insights into the shops, buildings and other features depicted.

If you recognize anyone in the photographs in this book, or if you have information not already included in the author's caption, do let us know. We would love to hear from you, and will try to publish it in future books or articles.

Our production team

Frith books are produced by a small dedicated team at offices in the converted Grade II listed 18th-century barn at Teffont near Salisbury, illustrated above. Most have worked with the Frith Collection for many years. All have in common one quality: they have a passion for the Frith Collection. The team is constantly expanding, but currently includes:

Jason Buck, John Buck, Douglas Burns, Ruth Butler, Heather Crisp, Isobel Hall, Hazel Heaton, Peter Horne, James Kinnear, Tina Leary, Hannah Marsh, Sue Molloy, Kate Rotondetto, Dean Scource, Eliza Sackett, Terence Sackett, Sandra Sanger, Lewis Taylor, Shelley Tolcher, Clive Wathen and Jenny Wathen.